D1459645

DuNG BeETLeS, SLuGS, LeEcHeS, and MoRE:
THE YUCKY ANIMAL BOOK

Alvin and Virginia
Silverstein
and
Laura Silverstein Nunn

Illustrated by
Gerald Kelley

Library of Congress Cataloging-in-Publication Data:

Silverstein, Alvin.
    Dung beetles, slugs, leeches, and more : the yucky animal book / by Alvin Silverstein,
Virginia Silverstein, and Laura Silverstein Nunn.
       p. cm. — (Yucky science)
    Summary: "Explores 'yucky' things animals do, including slime-producing animals,
blood-ingesting animals, and more"—Provided by publisher.
    Includes bibliographical references and index.
    ISBN 978-0-7660-3317-7
    1. Animal behavior—Juvenile literature. 2. Insects—Behavior—Juvenile literature.
3. Invertebrates—Behavior—Juvenile literature. I. Silverstein, Virginia B. II. Nunn, Laura
Silverstein. III. Title.
    QL751.5S553 2010
    590—dc22
                        2009012281

Printed in the United States of America

052010 Lake Book Manufacturing, Inc., Melrose Park, IL

10 9 8 7 6 5 4 3 2 1

To Our Readers: We have done our best to make sure all Internet Addresses in this book were
active and appropriate when we went to press. However, the author and the publisher have no
control over and assume no liability for the material available on those Internet sites or on other
Web sites they may link to. Any comments or suggestions can be sent by e-mail to comments@
enslow.com or to the address on the back cover.

♻ Enslow Publishers, Inc., is committed to printing our books on recycled paper. The paper
in every book contains 10% to 30% post-consumer waste (PCW). The cover board on the
outside of each book contains 100% PCW. Our goal is to do our part to help young people
and the environment too!

Illustration Credits: © 2009 Gerald Kelley, www.geraldkelley.com

Photo Credits: © Alasdair Thomson/iStockphoto.com, p. 31; Brandon Cole/Visuals
Unlimited, Inc., p. 11 (top); Eye of Science/Photo Researchers, Inc., p. 21; © Fred Bavendam/
Minden Pictures, p. 42; Dr. James L. Castner/Visuals Unlimited, Inc., p. 30; James McCullagh/
Visuals Unlimited, Inc., p. 11 (bottom); Joe McDonald/Visuals Unlimited, Inc., p. 34; © Lion
Hijmans/iStockphoto.com, p. 23; Nature's Images/Photo Researchers, Inc., p. 25; © Nick
Gordon/naturepl.com, p. 14; © Raymond Mendez/Animals Animals, p. 43; Scientifica/Visuals
Unlimited, Inc., p. 15; Shutterstock, p. 10.

Cover Illustration: © 2009 Gerald Kelley, www.geraldkelley.com

Enslow Publishers, Inc.
40 Industrial Road
Box 398
Berkeley Heights, NJ 07922
USA
      http://www.enslow.com

CONTENTS

What's Yucky?

Do you get grossed out when you spot a worm wriggling on the ground? What about when you see a slug clinging to the underside of a leaf? Would you ever touch one? Eew, slimy! Do you get the creeps when you see a spider? What if it was a really big, hairy spider, such as a tarantula? Yikes! Would you want to run the other way?

What makes an animal seem yucky to you? Slime is a popular answer. It feels so gross! Most people think bad smells are yucky, too. But in the animal world, how an animal looks, feels, smells, or behaves is a matter of survival. Slime helps keep a slug from drying out. It could also save its life. An animal looking for a meal will stay away if it doesn't want a mouthful of goo.

Do you think drinking blood is gross? Bedbugs, leeches, and ticks survive by drinking the blood of people and animals. A tick may drink so much blood that its flat body swells up like a fat, ripe grape.

Slithering snakes scare some people. But the hognose snake does something extra disgusting. It scares away its enemies by puking on itself and then playing dead. Just one whiff—yuck! The hognose snake isn't the only animal that uses puke as a weapon. Some kinds of birds will puke on any enemy that gets too close. That kind of defense wouldn't gross out a housefly or a vulture, though. They eat rotting meat and find stinky smells yummy, not yucky!

People may also disagree about what's yucky. Some people think insects are creepy, and wiggling worms are gross. In some parts of the world, though, people eat them! Many people think snakes and big, hairy spiders are yucky, but others enjoy keeping them as pets.

In this book, we'll find out more about some of nature's "yuckiest" critters.

slime
Time

FOLLOW THAT SLIME!

Slugs leave a trail of slime wherever they go. They glide along on a long, soft "foot" covered with sticky slime. This slime is mucus, made in the foot. Like a runny nose, the slug's foot keeps making mucus. The mucus helps to keep the slug from drying out. It also helps the slimy critter grip surfaces as it moves. The slug can crawl up and over rocks, stick fast to the underside of twigs or leaves, or climb up walls.

Have you ever seen a dried-up slug on the sidewalk? That's what happens when it gets caught out in the sun too long. Its protective mucus dries up, and the slug dies.

Snails vs. Slugs

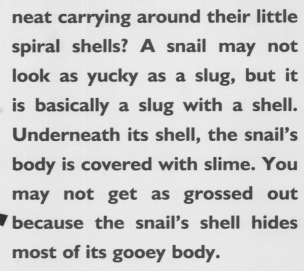

Do snails gross you out? Or do you think they look neat carrying around their little spiral shells? A snail may not look as yucky as a slug, but it is basically a slug with a shell. Underneath its shell, the snail's body is covered with slime. You may not get as grossed out because the snail's shell hides most of its gooey body.

A slug's slime has some other important uses as well. Some slugs squirt out a string of mucus from their tail end. When it is time to mate, a slug leaves a chemical in its slime trail that sends a signal to other slugs. They follow the trail straight to the slug that left it. When the two slugs get together, they hang from a rope of slime to mate.

Slime also makes a great weapon. Slugs can use their slime against predators—animals that want to eat them. A bird, for example, might have trouble holding on to the slippery body of a slug. Predators also know that a slimy feel and a yucky taste may be signs that something is not safe for them to eat.

Yikes! The banana slug is long and bright yellow, just like a banana. But you wouldn't want to eat this banana! When it feels threatened, the banana slug makes extra globs of slime. A predator that tries to eat it will get a mouthful of sticky goo.

UNDERWATER GOO

The hagfish is by far the number one champion slimeball. It looks like an eel, with a long, slippery body. It is not an eel, though. The hagfish is a fish with no jaws and no bones. Like a slug, its body is covered with thick, gooey mucus. But the hagfish makes a *lot* more sticky slime than a slug.

Slime is the hagfish's main defense against enemies. When this fish is bothered or frightened,

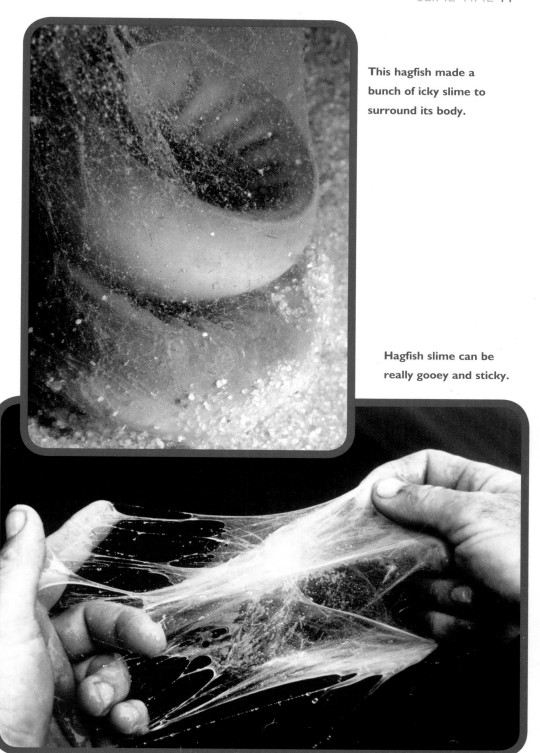

This hagfish made a bunch of icky slime to surround its body.

Hagfish slime can be really gooey and sticky.

thin streams of slime gush from its body. As soon as the slime hits the seawater, it quickly swells up. This happens so fast that predators are taken completely by surprise. Soon they are covered with huge, thick gobs of slime! That's enough to scare away any enemy. The slime can also clog the gills of underwater predators so that they can't breathe. Scientists who study hagfish say that this gooey fish can make as much as a gallon of slime at one time.

Neat Trick!

Can you guess how a hagfish cleans extra slime from its body? First it ties itself into a knot. Then it works this knot down its body, wiping off slime along the way. Now that's a neat trick!

CHAPTER TWO

A Taste for Blood

BLOODSUCKING VAMPIRE!

Vampires are only make-believe, aren't they? In scary stories, these "monsters" sneak around at night, sucking blood from humans. In reality, there is no such thing as vampires, but certain kinds of bats actually *do* have to drink blood to survive. For this reason, they are called vampire bats.

Just like the vampires in stories, vampire bats come out at night to feed. But vampire bats do not usually drink blood from humans. It *can* happen, but it's very rare! Vampire bats usually feed on blood from cows, pigs, horses, and birds. Usually the bats pick animals that are sleeping.

Vampire bats lick blood from a
wound after biting an animal.

Yikes! **Vampire bats can keep drinking blood from an animal for more than thirty minutes without waking it up. The victim doesn't feel a thing! That's because the bat's saliva contains a special chemical that makes the bite painless. The chemical also helps to keep the blood from thickening and healing the wound, so the bat can keep drinking.**

After flying circles around its snoozing victim, the vampire bat may land carefully on the animal's body. Or it may land nearby and creep silently forward. The bat then bites so quickly that the victim does not even wake up. A vampire bat doesn't actually *suck* blood. It makes a tiny cut with its razor-sharp teeth and then laps up the flowing blood with its tongue.

BLOODSUCKING WORMS

You don't want to go swimming in a lake or pond that has leeches. You may come out of the water with these wormlike creatures all over your body. They suck your blood—and they won't want to let go.

Leeches have suction cup mouths that attach to the skin of an animal.

DOCTOR! DOCTOR!

Doctors have been using leeches for about four thousand years! In the nineteenth century, leech treatments became very popular. Doctors often used leeches to treat many medical conditions. Today, doctors still sometimes use them!

Leeches are especially useful after surgery to reattach fingers or ears that have been cut or torn off in an accident. The surgeon carefully matches up the torn nerves and blood vessels and sews them back together. When blood vessels are damaged, blood tends to form thick lumps, called clots. The clots usually help your body stop bleeding after you get a cut or scrape. After surgery, though, blood clots may clog up small blood vessels, keeping blood from flowing through them. Without a blood supply, a reattached ear or finger could shrivel up and die.

The doctor places leeches onto the body part. The leeches suck out the extra blood from swollen areas and keep the blood flowing freely. Patients may get grossed out looking at the leeches attached to them, but they won't feel any pain. After surgery, when the swelling has gone down, the doctor removes the leeches.

A leech has a little suction cup at each end of its long body. It uses these suckers to attach itself to the skin of an animal. One sucker is the leech's mouth. The mouth has *three* jaws, each with sharp little teeth. As the leech sinks its jaws into the skin, it makes a little cut. Then it drips some saliva into the wound and starts slurping.

You don't feel a thing when a leech chomps down. Like a vampire bat's, the leech's saliva has chemicals that block pain and keep the blood flowing freely. The blood doesn't dry up, so the leech can drink as much as it wants.

NIGHT NIGHT. SLEEP TIGHT.

Do you think bedbugs are just a part of some made-up story? Well, that old bedtime saying— "Night, night. Sleep tight. Don't let the bedbugs bite"—is actually based on fact. Bedbugs really do bite people while they are sleeping.

Bedbugs have been found in hotels, motels, college dorms, homes, apartments, and shelters. These bloodsuckers are active mainly at night. During the daytime, they hide in places close to where people sleep. Their tiny, flat bodies make it easy for them to slip into little cracks in mattresses, box springs, bed frames, and headboards. When they leave their hiding places at night, they don't have to travel far to get their blood meal from sleeping humans.

CHAPTER THREE

Sloppy Eaters

UGH! THERE'S A FLY IN MY SOUP!

If a housefly landed on your dinner plate, you'd probably just shoo it away with your hand and go back to your meal. But do you know what happens when a fly lands on your food? Do you *really* want to know? You might not feel the same way about flies again. They are more than just annoying little pests. When it comes to food, flies are really disgusting eaters!

Houseflies smell and taste with tiny hairs that cover their legs and feet. They will fly around and stop frequently, checking out whatever they land on. When a housefly finds something "tasty," its table manners can get pretty gross. It does not

This is what a fly looks like under a microscope. It uses its mouthparts to make food into a soup it can drink.

have teeth, so it cannot bite or chew food. It's on a liquid-only diet. If a fly wants to feast on solid food, such as a sandwich, first it needs to turn it into a soupy mix. It does that by throwing up on what it wants to eat! Chemicals in a fly's saliva break down the food, making it soft and moist. Then the fly can suck it up with a long mouthpart that's shaped like a drinking straw.

If you think that's gross, think about where a fly's feet have been. Flies are not very picky about what they eat. They hang out in places such as garbage dumps, sewers, and fields with manure. They especially love to eat rotting meat, garbage, and poop! These kinds of things are covered with germs. Flies carry these germs with them wherever they go, so it's not surprising that flies can spread diseases to people when they land on their food.

What Stinks?

The dead-horse arum and the titan arum are plants whose flowers smell like rotting meat or fish. They smell so bad that some people have passed out after getting a whiff of them! These plants actually *attract* flies. Flies love rotting meat! Once inside the flower, the fly gets trapped by stiff hairs. But the fly isn't going to be the flower's meal. The flower needs its help. After a few days, the hairs shrivel up and the fly can escape, carrying the flower's pollen. The fly brings the pollen to other plants and helps them make new plants.

A spider injects its victim with poison before wrapping it in silk.

SPIDER SMOOTHIES

Most spiders build a silk web to catch their meal. They make the silk themselves, inside their bodies, and squirt it out their rear end. Once an insect gets trapped among a spiderweb's sticky threads, there's no escape. What happens next would terrify you if you were that poor struggling insect. The spider dashes over, injects a dose of venom (poison), and wraps its victim in silk.

The venom paralyzes the spider's victim to keep it from moving. This poison also turns the insect's insides into a soupy liquid.

When the spider gets hungry, it sucks the liquid from one of its handy silk-wrapped bundles, leaving only an empty shell. The ground under a spiderweb is usually dotted with the sucked-out remains of the spider's meals. Talk about sloppy eaters!

Tarantulas don't spin webs to catch their meals. These big, hairy spiders are hunters. They line their underground homes with silky threads and wait for their victims to come to them. Tarantulas eat insects, such as crickets or moths. They also eat small mice, birds, frogs, and even

Yikes! A tarantula's body and legs are covered with pointy hairs. The spider will kick or fling these hairs if it is scared or annoyed. The hairs have a chemical in them that will cause an itchy rash when they stick to an enemy's skin.

other spiders! They may wait four or five weeks between meals. When an insect or frog comes close, the tarantula pops out of its burrow, runs a few steps, and grabs its prey with its fangs. The fangs inject venom that paralyzes the prey and turns its insides into soup.

CRITTER-EATING PLANTS

Most plants make their own food, but some of them can catch and eat animals! Plants do not have teeth to chew their food, or a stomach to

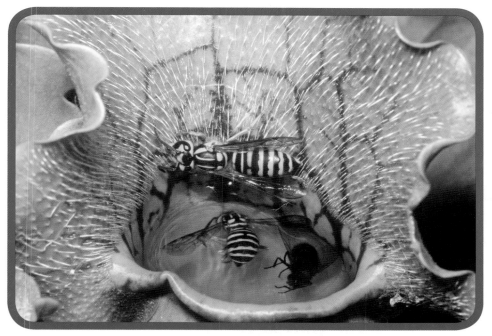

These yellowjackets were drowned in a pitcher plant. Unlike most plants, pitcher plants catch and eat animals for food.

digest it. Like spiders, these plants first turn the animals they eat into a soupy liquid.

The pitcher plant drowns its victims. The tube-shaped leaves of this plant look like jugs. Stiff hairs, pointing downward, grow on the inside of the leaves. Sweet nectar, oozing from the inside of the pitcher, lures insects. When an insect lands on this slippery nectar, it slides down into the plant. The stiff hairs stop the insect from escaping. The victim drowns in the pool of liquid at the bottom of the pitcher. Eventually, the plant breaks down the insect's body into a soup that it can use as food. The insect's tough outer shell doesn't break down, though. It sinks to the bottom of the pitcher. The pool of nectar in the bottom of a pitcher plant gradually fills with rotting insects and empty insect shells.

Oops! Sometimes small frogs hide inside pitcher plants. They eat the insects that are drawn to the plant's sweet nectar. If a frog slips and falls into the pool at the bottom, it becomes another meal for the plant!

Creepy Crawlies

OFF WITH YOUR HEAD!

Can you imagine any creature being able to live without its head? A cockroach can—not for just a second or a minute, but for weeks! How is that even possible? If a cockroach somehow loses its head, the neck can seal itself off. That way it doesn't bleed to death.

How can a cockroach function without a brain? It has nerves in each body segment. They allow it to do simple actions, such as standing, reacting to touch, and moving around.

A cockroach doesn't need a head to breathe, either. It doesn't breathe through a nose. Like all insects, it breathes through little holes in each

Would You Believe...?

A cockroach's head can also survive for a short time on its own, without a body. For a few hours, it will wave its antennae (feelers) back and forth.

body segment. The air gets sent directly to body tissues through a set of breathing tubes.

A headless cockroach can survive for a few weeks without eating. It lives on the food from its last meal. Eventually, it will run out of stored food and water—and die.

WATCH THEM WIGGLE!

Have you ever looked inside a trash can and found lots of tiny worms wriggling in the rotting garbage? Yuck! Although they look like worms, these little wrigglers are not really worms at all. They are actually larvae—the young form of an insect. Eventually, these tiny white larvae turn into flies. Fly larvae are called maggots.

The adult female fly lays her eggs where she knows her young will get plenty to eat. They come into the world with a ready-made buffet—a pile of rotting garbage, the body of a dead animal, an open wound, or even fresh animal poop! As soon as they hatch, the maggots turn into serious eating machines. Their mouths have tiny hooks that can

Flies lay their eggs where they know baby maggots will
have enough food to eat—even if that food is something
disgusting, like rotting garbage or *poop*!

Yikes! Doctors sometimes use live maggots to treat patients whose wounds are not healing right. In the patient's open wound, maggots feast only on the dead tissue. Once the wound is "cleaned," the doctor removes the maggots, and the wound has a better chance of healing.

easily tear into an animal's rotting body, garbage, or whatever else is in their path.

DIRT EATERS

Earthworms not only live in dirt, they eat it! They move by eating their way through the soil. They feed on bits of rotting plant and animal matter in the soil, as well as on tiny roundworms, bacteria, and fungi. The soil they eat goes straight through

Earthworms eat dirt and then poop it out as fertilizer, which helps plants grow.

the worms. Their poop acts like fertilizer, which makes the soil richer.

Like slugs, earthworms are very slimy. Their whole body is covered with mucus (the same slimy stuff as in your snot). An earthworm's slime helps keep it from drying out. It also helps the worm breathe. Oxygen from the soil passes into the slime, and then into the earthworm's body.

Would You Believe . . . ?

An earthworm can grow back lost body parts—depending on where it is cut. A worm can replace a lost tail, but it can't replace a lost head!

Cleanup Crew

NATURE'S POOPER SCOOPER

If you live on a farm or have ever visited one, you know that farm animals can make a lot of poop! Imagine trying to walk across a field and ending up with poop caked on your shoes. Dung beetles don't mind poop at all. In fact, *dung* is another name for poop. The dung beetle got its name because its whole life centers around dung. It eats poop, it works in poop, it sleeps in poop, and it breeds in poop.

Dung beetles bury the poop of animals, such as cows and elephants, and store it so that they can feed themselves and their families. The beetles roll poop into big round balls. One dung ball may weigh up to fifty times more than the beetle! Usually male beetles gather the poop, while their mates dig burrows. Once the dung balls are rolled into the burrows, the females lay their eggs in the poop. Wormlike larvae hatch from the eggs and eat the poop.

This dung beetle is rolling a big ball of POOP!

Would You Believe...?

Some dung beetles are really picky eaters. They will gather poop from only certain kinds of animals. Some feed only on elephant dung; others eat only cow dung or rabbit dung.

Some dung beetles try to steal dung balls from other dung beetles, so they have to work fast, sometimes burying loads of dung within hours.

The dung beetle is nature's pooper-scooper. Within a year, these hardworking insects can bury about half a ton of dung per acre! Without their help, the ground would be covered with poop.

GARBAGE COLLECTORS

When a deer gets hit by a car, its dead body can lie along the roadside for a long time. Eventually, the body starts to rot. Not only is it gross to look at, it can really stink, too. Luckily, nature has its own garbage collectors—vultures. While dung beetles help clean the earth of poop, these big birds help get rid of rotting dead animals. Vultures use their sense of smell to find food. To them, rotting meat smells *really* good!

Vultures aren't going to win any beauty contests. Unlike most other birds, North American vultures have no feathers on their head and neck. That's because of their messy eating habits. The vulture has to stick its head and neck inside an animal's carcass (dead body) to get to the meat. As it digs around, its skin picks up bits of blood and guts. Can you imagine what a mess it would be if its head were covered with feathers? The bird would have a much harder time keeping itself clean and free of the germs a rotting animal can carry.

As if their eating habits weren't gross enough, vultures have a yucky way of cleaning themselves.

Yikes! Any predator that gets too close to a turkey vulture or its nest had better watch out! This vulture is not afraid to throw up on demand. If the vomit hits the enemy in the face or eyes, it will sting. When the vulture throws up around its nest, the smell is so bad that most creatures don't want to get anywhere near it.

After finishing their meal, they poop on their legs! Their watery poop contains a very strong chemical that kills germs. In the summertime, vultures also poop on their legs to keep cool. The water in the vulture's poop evaporates (turns into a gas) and carries body heat off into the air.

CHAPTER SIX

Dirty Defenders

PLAY DEAD!

The hognose snake is famous for its dramatic "death scene." The snake opens its mouth and thrashes around as if it's in pain. Finally, it rolls onto its back with its mouth open and its tongue sticking out. It might even throw up. Then the inside of its mouth not only looks like rotting meat, but smells like it, too! P.U.! That is enough to turn away most enemies.

SHARPSHOOTERS

Small seabirds called fulmars lay their eggs on steep cliffs above the water. They eat small fish, squid, and other water animals. Fish guts and other garbage that fishing boats dump into the ocean are a real treat for these little seabirds. Fulmar parents leave their chicks alone when they fly off to find food. Other birds, such as gulls, may swoop down to gobble up the chicks. But fulmar chicks have a really gross defense. When threatened, they throw up. Stinky stomach oil squirts out—straight at the enemy. A fulmar chick can shoot its vomit as far as two or three meters (six to ten feet)!

Yikes! Fulmar chick puke not only stinks, it also sticks like superglue. It can glue an attacking predator's feathers together—and it won't wash off! The predator may even fall into the ocean and drown!

POOP SHOOTERS

Many caterpillars (the larvae of butterflies and moths) shoot out their poop. The poop balls fly through the air, over great distances. Shooting poop helps protect the caterpillars from their enemies, even though they don't actually shoot it *at* the enemies. These caterpillars live in shelters that they build by curling over a leaf and tying down the edges with silk to form a tent. If they just dropped their poop, it would pile up inside the shelter. Wasps that feed on caterpillars would smell the piles of poop and zero in on their prey. Shooting out poop balls sends the smelly chemicals away from the shelter. That makes it harder for the wasps to find where the caterpillars are hiding.

Sea cucumbers use poop shooting to gross out their enemies. These relatives of sea stars are shaped like cucumbers and have leathery skin covered with wartlike bumps and spines. They crawl along the ocean bottom and eat fish poop and bits of rotting stuff that drifts down through the water. Their food is pretty yucky to start with, so you can imagine how gross their poop is!

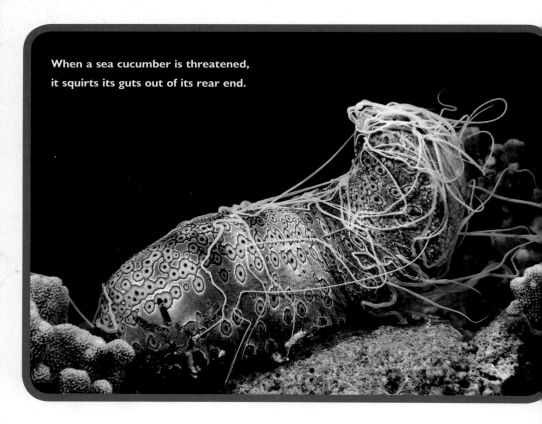

When a sea cucumber is threatened, it squirts its guts out of its rear end.

These creatures don't just shoot poop. When a sea cucumber is threatened by a fish, crab, or other enemy, it squirts part of its guts out through its rear end. The predator may get tangled in the sticky, smelly guts. Or it may decide that sea cucumbers are just too yucky to eat. If part of a sea cucumber does get eaten, it just regrows the parts it lost.

EEW! BLOOD!

If a horned lizard is attacked, it has a tricky defense. It can squirt a stream of blood from its eye, straight at the attacker! Only a few

A horned lizard can squirt blood out of its eyes to defend against an attacker.

Would You Believe . . . ?

A horned lizard can squirt blood up to three feet (about one meter)!

kinds of horned lizards can do this. They have special pouches underneath their eyes that fill up with blood. The predator is not only confused by the attack, it is also grossed out by the blood's disgusting taste.

The world is filled with lots of interesting, yucky animals. We've described only a handful of them. Which ones gross you out the most? Are they the slimy critters or the bloodsuckers? What about the ones that fling poop or shoot out their guts to scare away enemies? Some of these animals may sound really weird, but their yucky features often help them to survive.

WORDS TO KNOW

clot A solid lump of blood that can stop blood flow.

dung Poop.

evaporate To change from a liquid to a gas.

larva The young, wormlike form that hatches from the egg of many insects.

maggot The larva of a fly.

mucus A slimy substance produced by an animal's glands to provide moisture and protection.

predator An animal that hunts, kills, and eats other animals.

saliva Spit; a liquid that keeps the mouth moist and helps start digestion.

venom Poison.

vomit To throw up or puke; also, stomach contents that are forced out during vomiting.

FURTHER READING

Goldish, Meish. *Disgusting Hagfish.* New York: Bearport Publishing Co., 2008.

Houran, Lori Haskins. *Bloody Horned Lizard.* New York: Bearport Publishing Co., 2008.

Kravetz, Jonathan. *Cockroaches.* New York: PowerKids Press, 2006.

Miller, Connie Colwell. *Disgusting Animals.* Mankato, Minn.: Capstone Press, 2007.

Rosenberg, Pam. *Ack! Icky, Sticky, Gross Stuff Underground.* Mankato, Minn.: Child's World, 2007.

INTERNET ADDRESSES

Discovery Kids: The Yuckiest Site on the Internet. "Yucky Roach World."

<http://yucky.discovery.com/flash/roaches/
    index. html>

Popular Science. "Nature's Grossest Creatures."

<http://www.popsci.com/gross>

WhaleTimes. "Hagfish Day."

<http://www.whaletimes.org/HagfishDay.htm>

Index